A Note to Parents and Teachers

DK READERS is a compelling program for beginning readers, designed in conjunction with leading literacy experts.

Beautiful illustrations and superb full-color photographs combine with engaging, easy-to-read stories to offer a fresh approach to each subject in the series. Each DK READER is guaranteed to capture a child's interest while developing his or her reading skills, general knowledge, and love of reading.

The five levels of DK READERS are aimed at different reading abilities, enabling you to choose the books that are exactly right for your child:

Pre-level 1—Learning to read
Level 1—Beginning to read
Level 2—Beginning to read alone
Level 3—Reading alone
Level 4—Proficient readers

The "normal" age at which a child begins to read can be anywhere from three to eight years old, so these levels are only a general guideline.

No matter which level you select, you can be sure that you are helping your child learn to read, then read to learn!

LONDON, NEW YORK,
MUNICH, MELBOURNE, AND DELHI

Created by Tall Tree Ltd

For DK
Editor Laura Gilbert
Production Claire Pearson
DTP/Designer Dean Scholey
Picture Researcher Sarah Pownall
Picture Library Harriet Mills
Cover art by Jim Lee and Scott Williams

First American Edition, 2005
Published in the United States by
DK Publishing, Inc.
375 Hudson Street
New York, New York 10014

05 06 07 08 10 9 8 7 6 5 4 3 2 1

Library of Congress Cataloging-in-Publication Data

Hibbert, Clare, 1970-
Green Lantern's book of inventions / written by Clare Hibbert.--
1st American ed.
p. cm. -- (Dk readers. Level 4)
Includes index.
ISBN 0-7566-1012-5 (plc) -- ISBN 0-7566-1013-3 (pb)
1. Inventions--Juvenile literature. I. Title. II. Dorling Kindersley readers.
4, Proficient readers.
T48.H382 2004
600--dc22

2004017130

Color reproduction by Media Development and Printing Ltd, UK
Printed and bound in China by L Rex Printing Co., Ltd.

The publisher would like to thank the following for their kind permission
to reproduce their images:
Position key: c=center; b=bottom; l=left; r=right; t=top
DK Images: British Airways 42b; Tina Chambers/National Maritime
Museum, London, and IFREMER, Paris 39t; Christopher and Sally Gable
29b; Heidi Grassley 6b; Imperial War Museum 25b; Dave King 15t;
Richard Leeney/Courtesy of Search and Rescue Hovercraft, Richmond,
British Columbia 35t; Richard Leeney/Courtesy of the Fire crew at Logan
Airport, East Boston, Massachusetts 21l; NASA 31b; Susanna Price 17t.
NASA: 47b. Rex Features: Nils Jorgensen 12b.
Science Photo Library: Hank Morgan 18b.
All other photographs © Dorling Kindersley.
For further information see: www.dkimages.com

Dorling Kindersley would like to thank the following artists for their
contribution to this book: Bob Almond, Brent Anderson, Terry Austin,
Brandon Badeaux, Darryl Banks, Chris Batista, Dougie Braithwaite, Norm
Breyfogle, M. D. Bright, Sergio Cariello, Keith Champagne, Dan Davis,
John Dell, Dale Eaglesham, Wayne Faucher, Drew Geraci, Vince
Giarrano, Dave Gibbons, Dan Green, Adam Hughes, Jamal Igle, Dave
Johnson, Jeff Johnson, Michael Kaluta, Leonard Kirk, Jim Lee, Rob Leigh,
Mark Lipka, John Lowe, Doug Mahnke, Tom Mandrake, Adriana Melo,
Lee Moder, Tom Nguyen, Cary Nord, Jerry Ordway, Yanick Paquette, Paul
Pelletier, Brandon Peterson, Howard Porter, Rodney Ramos, Robin Riggs,
Craig Rousseau, Vince Russell, Bill Sienkiewicz, Romeo Tanghal, Sal
Velluto, Chip Wallace, Bob Wiacek, Scott Williams, and Al Williamson.

Discover more at
www.dk.com

Contents

DK READERS

PROFICIENT
4
READERS

JLA GREEN LANTERN'S BOOK OF INVENTIONS

Written by Clare Hibbert

DK

Meet Green Lantern

Alan Scott
Green Lantern Alan Scott made his own ring from the metal of a magic lantern he found near Gotham City.

Hal Jordan
Probably the greatest Green Lantern of all time, Hal Jordan helped found the JLA.

Greetings! I am Green Lantern, holder of the most awesome invention in the Universe—the power ring of the Guardians who live on the planet Oa. The ring uses green "hard light" to create anything I can imagine, giving me superpowers to protect Earth from all kinds of harm.

Inventions are great because they give us the power to achieve things that would have seemed impossible not so long ago. Today, we build inventions that save lives, travel through space, and give us information at the speed of light.

Every invention needs an inventor—the person who figured out how to give us that extra power. Inventors are usually very determined people who know a lot about science.

Inventors work alone, or in teams, like the super heroes of the Justice League of America (JLA).

You will learn about exciting inventions and discover those that are used by the JLA—and by our enemies. Follow me!

Guy Gardner and John Stewart Guy and John were temporary Green Lanterns. Guy retired to become the super hero Warrior and John now serves with the JLA.

The current Green Lantern is Kyle Rayner, a graphic artist who was given a ring by the Guardian Ganthet.

Shining lights

The power of sight is very important for humans. Some of our earliest inventions were made to increase our ability to see, by making light during the hours of darkness. For instance, torches were invented over 30,000 years ago.

Rings of power
Green Lanterns possess rings of power, which can create any objects their wearers can imagine. However, the rings do not work against anything that is yellow. They are designed with this weakness so their wearers do not become too powerful.

A lighthouse sends out powerful beams of light, letting sailors know where the coast is.

Cave people burned bundles of sticks dipped in animal fat. These lit up the caves while early artists painted pictures on the walls. You can still see sooty marks from the flames on the ceilings of these ancient homes.

Lighthouses were invented about 2,500 years ago. Modern ones each have their own pattern of flashes, which is marked on maps. When sailors see them at night, they can figure out where they are. The world's tallest, located in Yokohama, Japan, can be seen from 20 miles (32 kilometres) away.

A recent great invention in lighting was the lightbulb, invented by US scientist Thomas Edison in 1878. Lightbulbs use an electric current to make a very thin metal wire, called a filament, glow brightly.

Recharger
A Green Lantern's ring has to be recharged every 24 hours by contact with a magic lantern. The lantern draws its power from the Central Power Battery on Oa, the Guardians' home world.

Laser beams

Light is not just for sight—it has other uses, too. Between 1958 and 1960, scientists discovered how to create a superpowered beam of light. The first working laser was built by American physicist Theodore Maiman in 1960.

Lasers produce a sharp, focused beam of light. One type of laser beam is made when light is flashed inside a tube of ruby crystals. The atoms in the crystals become excited and produce tiny bursts of light called photons. These pass through the tube to a mirror at the end in a straight laser beam.

Laser beams can cut through hard materials such as metals. Today, lasers are everywhere— for example, they make and play your CDs and DVDs.

Lasers even can improve poor eyesight. The beam of a laser can be used to reshape the lens at the front of the human eye— and the patient never needs to wear glasses or contact lenses again!

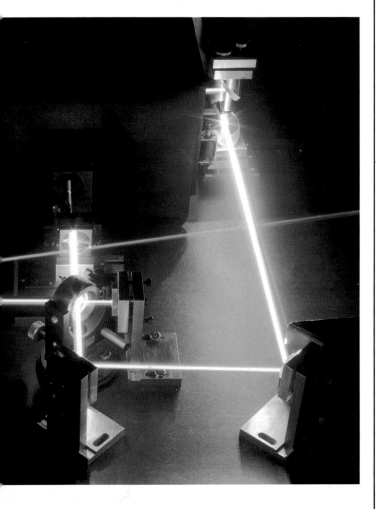

Super ring
The special ring given to Kyle Rayner by Ganthet only runs out of power after heavy use. The 24-hour time limit does not apply to this unique ring.

The beam of a laser reflects from mirror to mirror in this laboratory.

Catching light

People once had to rely on their memories to recall what they had seen—or make drawings. It was not until the 1820s that a French inventor called Nicéphore Niépce discovered a way of capturing a realistic image of what he saw. Niépce's first camera took almost a whole day to take a picture.

Paparazzi
When he became Green Lantern, Kyle Rayner was going out with a newspaper photographer named Alex DeWitt. She was the first journalist to take pictures of the new Green Lantern.

In 1839, another Frenchman, Louis-Jacques-Mandé Daguerre, perfected a way of making high-quality images on a metal plate in just 20 minutes. His daguerreotype pictures became very popular.

By 1888, the Eastman Kodak Company in the US was selling cameras for home use. These cameras contained a roll of film, which could catch images quickly and easily.

In 1892, American inventors Thomas Edison and William Dickson used a roll of film in a camera that could take hundreds of pictures a minute. When these were fed through a light projector, motion pictures—movies—were born.

Cameras that record images onto film have a shutter that exposes the film to light. The total amount of light entering the camera is called the exposure.

Dark duels
The League of Super-Heroes battled against the evil Servants of Darkness before meeting the Servants' powerful master, Darkseid.

Digital images

Traditional photographs and movie camera images were not easy to copy. Creating each print of an original image needed a lot of work and special chemicals.

Digital technology makes copying much easier. Digital cameras convert light into information a computer can read, copy, and display.

Laser rescue
The scarlet-clad Valor rescued the Green Lantern Alia from her battle with the Unimaginable by blasting the evil being with laser light.

Computer game designers build virtual wire-frame objects and then add a skin of digital images.

Digital cameras use a CCD, or "charge-coupled device," to detect light. Canadian Willard Boyle and American George Smith developed the first CCD in 1969. A CCD is made up of thousands of microscopic "buckets" that fill up with an electrical charge when light hits them. The charges are passed along the row of buckets and counted by a computer.

The computer figures out what the image is, and rebuilds it with tiny squares of light that are called pixels.

Digital images can be copied as easily as any computer file. They can be sent down a telephone line, over the internet, or even via satellite.

Maser by name Hal Jordan's cousin Harold, or Air Wave, was also nicknamed the Maser. He had the power to convert his body into energy and travel from place to place via radio waves.

Making sound

Until 1877, music had to be created live in front of its audience. Then, Thomas Edison found a way to record sound. He called his invention the phonograph, from the ancient Greek for "sound writing."

Edison's machine used a telephone mouthpiece and a needle. Talking into the mouthpiece made the needle wobble, and scratch a line across a wax cylinder. Another needle wobbling over the bumps made by the first would make the telephone mouthpiece recreate the noises.

Eventually, better sound was produced by records. The first were made from wax, and later ones from a type of plastic called vinyl. However, records wear out with use, and can become scratched.

Angel cry
The Winged Wonder Zauriel has the power of an angel's voice. His cry is so powerful that it can shatter almost any solid object.

Nasty noise
Deranged arch-enemy Sonar implanted gruesome electronic circuitry (wiring) under his own skin. He wanted to use his own body to generate deadly sound waves.

Superb sound arrived with digital recording. The compact disc, or CD, was invented in 1980 by the electronics company Philips. Sounds are encoded onto a CD in computer language. Copies of the recording are just as clear as the original.

Tele-twins
Alan Scott's two children, the lovely Jade and the wicked Obsidian (above), were telepathically connected to each other. Each knew whenever the other one was in distress.

In 1838, American inventor Samuel Morse developed Morse Code. This changed numbers and letters into dots and dashes, allowing messages to be sent over early telegraph networks or by flashing lights.

Distant voices

In 1792, French engineer Claude Chappe invented semaphore—a way of sending messages along a line of lookouts. Operators moved two sticks into different positions in order to create coded signals that could be passed from horizon to horizon.

Semaphore only worked on clear days, when operators could see long distances. It was replaced with electric cables in the 1840s, which used the dots and dashes of Morse Code to send messages. By 1858, this telegraph system could carry signals between Europe and America.

In 1875, Scottish inventor Alexander Graham Bell found a way to send voices along cables—he invented the telephone. Telephone networks were gradually set up all around the world.

Until the 1930s telephone users still required an operator to connect them to the number they were dialing. Soon, the sheer number of users required a fully automated system.

In the 1950s, the US Army needed computers that could speak to each other over long distances. Inventors came up with a device called the modem. This machine converts computer language into signals that can pass through telephone networks. This amazing invention led to the creation of the world wide web or internet.

Sacrifice
Jade inherited the power of the magical entity called the Starheart from Alan Scott, her father. She gave up this power to save the life of Kyle Rayner.

Green fuse
Jade's villainous mother, Thorn, passed on her powers to her daughter. Jade only discovered these powers, which harness the energy of plants, after losing the power of the Starheart.

Automatic ears

The first machine that could analyze the human voice was probably the phonautograph, or "speech signature" machine. It was invented by French scientist Leon Scott in 1857. The phonautograph converted vibrations made by a human voice into squiggles that were drawn on a sheet or tube.

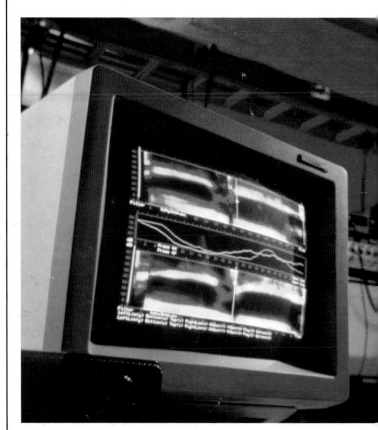

This computer is comparing the sound waves made by the voices of various people.

It was used to teach deaf people to speak and for studying languages, but it needed a human operator to interpret the squiggles.

In 1952, a primitive computer at Bell Laboratories in New Jersey was trained to recognize spoken numbers from zero to nine. Modern personal computers can run software that recognizes 98 words out of 100, if they are spoken clearly enough.

Computers can also analyze the sound of a voice to identify a person. The chips needed are so small that one company, called Beepcard, has built them into a credit card. The card checks the sound of its owner's voice before allowing the transaction.

Repaying the favor
Kyle Rayner restored Jade's Starheart power to her while he was in his incarnation as Ion, the all-powerful force.

The Fists of the Guardians—robots with the power to arrest Green Lanterns.

Sharp suits

Keeping trim
Professor Emil Hamilton made Superman an electronic suit after the hero's body was accidentally transformed into pure energy. The suit helped Superman hold himself together.

Some inventions improve everyday items, such as clothing. All clothing was made of completely natural materials until the end of the 19th century. In 1884, French chemist Hilaire Chardonnet invented a process for creating artificial silk.

An improved method for making artificial fabrics was invented in Britain in 1892. The fiber was called viscose rayon. Nylon, a general-purpose artificial fiber, followed in 1938. It was used to create the first bulletproof vests, called flak jackets. Modern clothing can be bulletproof and fireproof.

Inventions also keep our clothes on! Swede Gideon Sundback invented the zipper in 1914, based on earlier ideas by American engineer Whitcomb Judson.

Then, in 1941, Swiss engineer Georges de Mestral wondered why plant burrs stuck to his trousers and to his dog. He studied the surface of these plant parts, and realized that he could copy it to make sticky fabrics. In 1951, he patented Velcro.

Dark mystery
Nobody knows who or what Dark Lantern is, or why he/it hunts and kills Green Lanterns. Dark Lantern's body is covered with mysterious runelike symbols.

The fabric of this firefighter's suit has been treated with flame-retarding chemicals. It also has a silver-effect coating that deflects heat.

Keeping time

For most of human history, it was difficult to tell the exact time. This made it impossible to measure speed and journey times accurately, and caused a lot of waiting around!

The position of the Sun in the sky gives a clue to the time of day. The first clocks were sundials. These show the Sun's position by measuring where a shadow falls, but they only work in direct sunlight.

Time foes
Time-tinkering villains Calendar Man, Chronos, Clock King (above), and Time Commander teamed up to cause chronological chaos as the Time Foes. They were defeated by Team Titans.

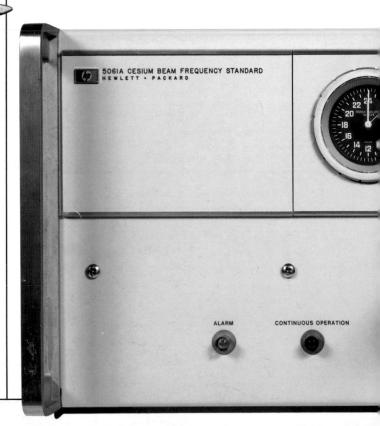

In the 1650s, Dutch physicist Christiaan Huygens invented a clock with a swinging pendulum. This kept time accurately enough to make it worth having minute hands for the first time.

The most accurate clocks are atomic clocks. The first, built in 1948, was only accurate to within three seconds per year. By 1959, atomic clocks were accurate to within one second every 2,000 years.

History
Abin Sur was Green Lantern for sector 2814 from the middle of the 19th century. He had been a professor of history on his home world of Ungara.

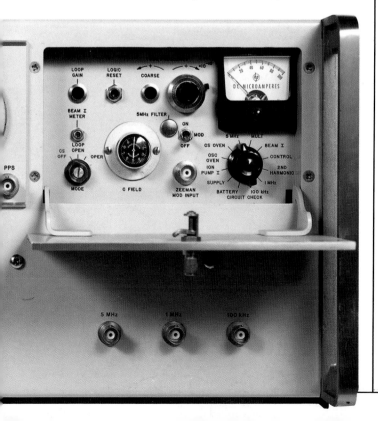

An atomic clock like this one keeps time to the oscillations, or wobbles, of an atom's nucleus.

Armaments

In ancient warfare, a soldier's strength and skill determined how much damage his sword, spear, or arrow could do to the enemy. Later, inventions such as catapults allowed a lot of power to be put into a weapon, which could then be released suddenly.

Gunpowder and missiles were invented in China in about 1000 CE. Chinese warfare soon developed metal guns and cannons, which were used by the Mongol Empire and brought to Europe in about 1250.

In 1887, Swedish inventor Alfred Nobel invented cordite, a clean, high-explosive gunpowder that allowed guns to fire many rounds without jamming with soot. By 1914, rifles were so powerful that soldiers needed thick armor plate to protect themselves against bullets.

In the blood
Guy Gardner's Vuldarian ancestors were a powerful warrior race. When his powers began to show, he became Warrior.

The first armored tank went into action in 1915.

Since 1939, modern warfare on land and at sea is usually decided by which side has the most powerful air force. Long-range bombers destroy enemy defenses with little risk to the attackers.

Qward thunder
The Weaponers of Qward, an evil antimatter species, equip their armies of Thunderers with qwa-bolts. These are yellow bolts of lightning-like energy that devastate all they touch.

This Russian tank has a curved turret that was designed to deflect missiles.

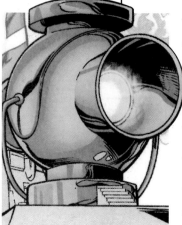

Natural power

To exceed the limits of human strength, we need to use power from other parts of nature. The first power harnessed by people was that of animals, such as horses and cattle.

Water-driven machines were probably first used in Greece in about 100 BCE. The Romans used water wheels to drive millstones that ground grain into flour, saving many hours of back-breaking work.

Central power
The 3,600 lanterns across the Universe draw their energy from the Central Power Battery on the Guardians' home world, Oa. The Guardians made the battery to contain the magic powers of the Universe.

Vast "wind farms" like this one have become a feature of the landscape in many countries. The propellers generate electricity from the power of the wind.

Water mills were often built over a small dam across a stream. The pond caused by the dam forced water more powerfully through the wheel. This water power is still used today in huge hydroelectric dam projects in places such as Niagara Falls.

In about 700 CE, the Persians began using wind power to help mill their grain. Their invention of the windmill gradually evolved over centuries to become the modern wind turbine, which creates electricity.

Parallax
When Hal Jordan conquered Oa in his quest for ultimate power, he merged with the Central Power Battery and became Parallax.

Sinestro
Disgraced Green Lantern Sinestro tried to stop Hal Jordan from blowing up the Central Power Battery.

Making power

Burning natural resources is another way to release useful energy. Wood fires kept us warm for thousands of years and allowed us to cook food.

Coal power was discovered in China in about 200 BCE, and in the Roman Empire shortly afterward. The Romans burned coal to smelt metals and to heat buildings.

Modern coal power stations can produce enough electricity for about five million people—and burn more than 35,000 tons of coal a day. This gives off a gas called carbon dioxide, which can be harmful to the environment.

Heavy burden
Kyle Rayner gained super energies to become Ion, the most powerful being in the Universe. He also began to lose his humanity, and found it impossible to sleep, to be in just one place, or to care about his friends.

In a coal power station, coal is burned to heat water. This creates steam that spins a turbine to drive a generator to create electricity. The steam is changed back to water inside giant cooling towers. Some water vapor escapes into the air in great white clouds.

The first nuclear power stations were built in the 1950s in the US and Russia. They do not produce carbon dioxide, but the fuels they use are radioactive. This means that they can stay dangerous for hundreds of years.

Ion storm
Kyle eventually gave up being Ion. He channeled his energy into creating a new race of Guardians who emerged from a new Central Power Battery.

Thrust

Sometimes people need power on the move. Among the first engine vehicles was a steam-powered tractor, built by French inventor Joseph Cugnot in 1769. It had a top speed of 2.5 mph (4 km/h)!

Steam engines are heavy in comparison with the power they can create. Inventors call this a poor power-to-weight ratio. Steam was best for powering huge trains and ships, but not small vehicles.

The Belgian Étienne Lenoir invented the internal combustion engine in 1859. This burned its fuel inside the engine and had a much better power-to-weight ratio than steam engines. German engineers Gottlieb Daimler and Karl Benz attached an internal combustion engine to a vehicle and invented the car in 1886.

Internal combustion is still too weak to blast a vehicle into space. Liquid-fuel rocket engines were first developed in the 1920s. They burn huge amounts of fuel and ride the blast into space.

Jetpack
If he's ever in a tricky situation, Green Lantern can always summon up a light-powered jetpack to blast his way clear of trouble.

The space shuttle is strapped to two huge rocket boosters and a giant fuel tank, which blast it into orbit.

The wheel

One of the most important inventions of all time is the wheel. It is used in activities as different as making pottery and controlling computer games. But its most widespread use is in transportation.

The first solid-wooden cartwheels were made in about 3500 BCE. By 2000 BCE, lighter wheels with wooden spokes had been invented for chariots.

Drunk driver
Hal Jordan did some stupid things with cars. He was in prison for drunk driving when Sinestro first visited him to begin Hal's training as a Green Lantern.

The first trucks had wheels made of solid rubber. Eventually, wheels were given inner tubes filled with air, like those on this dump truck.

MM 444

The spoked wheel is still used today on bicycles and motorcycles.

Wooden wheels did not cope well with the stress of hard surfaces. Metal bands were nailed around wheels to prevent them from splintering. When the railroads arrived, engineers finally began to rethink the wheel.

Wheels made of solid metal were first used on trains in the 1840s. Metal wheels covered in rubber were needed for cars and motorcycles.

American inventor Charles Goodyear developed vulcanized rubber in 1844— paving the way for the first rubber tires.

Mega fist
One of Kyle's earliest battles as Green Lantern was against the mighty Mongul. Kyle delivered his knockout blow by conjuring up a freight train that slammed Mongul into the floor. Even Superman was impressed!

Wheel free

Wheels are good for rolling, but when the ground is wet or bumpy, wheels can get stuck. Inventors have come up with some cool ways to solve this problem.

People have known for a long time that it is easier to slide than to roll on snow, ice, and slippery surfaces. The first ice-skates and skis were invented as far back as 2500 BCE!

In 1959, Canadian tycoon Joseph-Armand Bombardier invented the personal snowmobile, or Skidoo. Powered by a motorcycle engine, it used steerable skis at the front and had a rubberized caterpillar track to grip the snow.

Wheelchairs face a different challenge, and have trouble coping with stairs and other obstacles.

Tube travel
When the Justice League set up embassies across the world, they installed a system of teleporter tubes to link each embassy.

Hovercraft are able to move across land and water. They glide on a cushion of air that is trapped beneath the hull's inflatable rubber skirt.

Horsepower
In some places, having wheels just won't get you from A to B. In this situation, a Green Lantern can summon up any form of transportation he or she wishes, including a galloping horse.

In 2004, Japanese inventors created "legchairs." These walk on legs and are able to step rather than roll.

A walking truck was built in 1967 by American engineer Ralph Moser. Instead of wheels, the truck had a leg at each corner. A driver moved pedals to control each leg.

Sailing the waves

People have always found ways of crossing the sea. Early vessels were probably no more than simple rafts, which the first humans used to float from island to island.

The first seagoing ships in recorded history were built by the ancient Egyptians in about 2000 BCE. Their ships had square linen sails, as well as paddles to use when the wind blew in the wrong direction.

Polynesian seafarers used boats to explore the Pacific islands. Historians guess that they began building huge canoes, paired together, in about 500 BCE. The battleships of the ancient Greeks and Romans who sailed the Mediterranean were huge rowing boats.

Sea prince
As a child, Aquaman was exiled from the undersea kingdom of Atlantis, where he had been the boy prince Orin. He was adopted by a lighthouse keeper who taught him about life on dry land.

Up to 200 slaves rowed the oars to push the ship through the water.

Among the biggest wooden ships ever made were the junks sailed by the Chinese admiral Cheng Ho in the 1400s.

Second chance
Aquaman was once defeated so badly that he lost all his powers. However, the Lady of the Lake revived him and gave him magical abilities as "The Waterbearer."

This racing yacht gets its speed by turning its side to the wind. Its crew must lean in the opposite direction to stop it from blowing over!

Sea power

The first small metal ships were built in about 1820. In 1862, iron ships went into battle for the first time, in the American Civil War. The *Monitor* and the *Merrimack* fought to a draw.

Container ships were invented in the 1950s. They carry cargo in standard-sized metal boxes that can be loaded directly from a ship onto a truck or a train.

Transporting oil needs extra care. The first double-skinned oil tanker was built in 1992. The inner skin saves the oil from spilling if the outer skin is punctured.

The first attempt to travel under the water came in 1623, when Dutch scientist Cornelius Drebbel built a submarine, powered by oarsmen.

The mini-submarine Nautile *can operate at a depth of 3.7 miles (6 kilometers). It is equipped with cameras and robotic arms, and can carry a crew of three.*

German engineer Wilhelm Bauer created the first three-man sub in 1850. It sank on its second trip, but Bauer built another submarine in 1855, the *Sea Devil*. He used it to entertain a crowd by taking a four-man brass band underwater!

Undersea city Poseidonis is a mobile, undersea city controlled by Aquaman. It is built on a living rock that was formerly the spaceship home of an alien intelligence.

Flying machines

People have wanted the power of flight for thousands of years. In the ancient Greek legend of Icarus, an inventor's son used feathers stuck together with wax to fly, but the Sun melted the wax and Icarus plunged to Earth.

In about 1485, Italian genius Leonardo da Vinci drew designs for different flying machines, including sketches of birds' wings, a glider, and a "helicopter" that used a giant corkscrew to rise into the air.

French brothers Joseph and Étienne Montgolfier built the first hot-air balloon in 1783. After trials that involved sending animals for a ride, the first manned flight was made.

Stealth bombshell
When his copilot Vince Hardy tried to steal an experimental stealth bomber, Hal Jordan battled to stop him. Hal lost his job with the US Air Force after the bomber crashed and Hardy got away.

Easy to maneuver, helicopters took time to develop. The first practical one flew in 1936.

Backup wings
Green Lanterns gain the power of flight from their power ring. However, Tomar-Re, the Xudarian Green Lantern of Sector 2813, has natural wings, too, which he keeps tucked away.

In 1891, German inventor Otto Lilienthal built a glider that could carry a man through the air, even without power. His glider created lift like a modern aircraft's wing.

American bicycle mechanic Orville Wright and his brother Wilbur built the first powered plane, *The Flyer*, in 1903.

Noble knight
Emerald Knight
was one of the
Circle of Fire
Green Lanterns.
The Circle of
Fire is a
Green Lantern
storyline.

Alexandra DeWitt,
Kyle's murdered
girlfriend,
reappeared as
a Circle of Fire
Green Lantern.

Faster than sound

Once the Wright brothers had
shown how a machine that was
heavier than air could fly, the age
of flight could begin.

French cyclist Paul Cornu
became the world's first helicopter
pilot in 1907. He barely lifted off the
ground! In 1909, French pilot Louis
Blériot took 37 minutes to fly his
plane across the English Channel,
becoming the first person to do so.

A year later, another Frenchman, Henri Fabre, flew the first aircraft able to land on water.

The next major invention in flight was the jet engine, developed by British and German engineers during World War II. Jet engines suck in air, mix fuel into it, and vent the "exploding" exhaust gases from the rear of the engine, making thrust. Jet engines pushed American pilot George Welch through the sound barrier in 1953, just five years after a rocket plane had made the first supersonic flight.

The Concorde was the world's first and last supersonic passenger jet. It was taken out of service in 2003.

Cold light
The Circle of Fire's robot Green Lantern was created from Kyle Rayner's powers of logic and rationality. It was programmed to get rid of evil.

Space explorers

Inventors gave us the power to explore space. The first telescope used for studying space belonged to the Italian astronomer Galileo. He built it in 1609 after hearing rumors of a similar instrument made in Holland. Within a year, Galileo had used it to make star maps and had become the first person to see the moons of the planet Jupiter.

English scientist Isaac Newton invented a whole new type of mathematics called calculus, in about 1670. Calculus allowed Newton to figure out how planets and comets move around the Sun.

Knowing how space worked only encouraged people to get clear of the Earth's atmosphere and explore the Solar System!

Double green
J'onn J'onzz is a green man from Mars, and one of the JLA's founders. He is one of just two Martians that are still alive.

Rockets that could lift robots or people into space were invented in the USA and Russia after World War II.

In April 1961, the Russian team of inventors were the first to launch a man into space. Yuri Gagarin orbited the Earth for one hour and 48 minutes before returning safely to a hero's welcome.

Evil green
The other living Martian is the mad one who destroyed Martian civilization – Ma'alefa'ak (Malefic). He still wants to complete his project by killing J'onzz.

Launched in 1972, space probe Pioneer 10 sent back the first detailed images of Jupiter. In 1983, it became the first craft to travel beyond the Solar System's outermost known planet, which, at that time, was Pluto.

Stations in space

In the 1970s, Russian and American research teams tested ways to live and work in small space capsules orbiting above the Earth. In 1986, Russia began to build *Mir*, a much larger space station. *Mir*'s sections were launched into space separately, and assembled in orbit.

Space stations became easier to build with the help of the US's reusable spacecraft, the space shuttle, first launched in 1981.

Life in orbit depends on thousands of new inventions. NASA invented a toilet that works in the weightlessness of orbit, and Velcro straps were used by sleeping astronauts to stick themselves down.

Space tricks
When Sinestro was training Hal Jordan, he scolded the younger Lantern for weaving through a meteor shower! Sinestro thought Lanterns should not use their power for amusement.

Free-floating crumbs could damage equipment, so different types of packaging were invented to deliver food out of a tube, like toothpaste.

Spacecraft and spacesuits gave astronauts the power to explore another world, the Moon, in person in 1969. These days, we use robot probes to investigate the planets.

Hitch a ride
Not all of the JLA members can fly through space. Those who can't use a small squadron of Jump Shuttles. The squadron has small craft for one pilot and larger ships to carry the whole of the JLA.

Working in a weightless environment takes some getting used to. Without weight the body begins to lose its muscle strength, so astronauts must exercise on special machines to stay in shape while in orbit.

Glossary

burr
The prickly seed head or seedcase of a plant. It is designed to stick to an animal's fur, so that the seed will be carried a long way from the parent plant.

chip
Short for microchip. A tiny circuit that carries computer data or information.

chronological
To do with time.

digital
Describes data that is stored as a series of numbers that can be recognized by a computer.

electric current
Movement of electrical energy. This usually flows along a wire.

embassy
Home to an ambassador who is the representative of a nation or an organization in a foreign country.

encode
To convert a normal message into a code.

hydroelectric dam
A barrier across a river that traps water. This water then flows through pipes to turn turbines and produce electricity.

junk
A type of sailing vessel that comes from China and the far east. It usually has a high rear, or poop deck, and uses square sails.

millstone
A flat, round stone used in a mill for grinding grain into flour.

ore
A lump of rock that contains metal.

pendulum
A weight hung so that it can swing freely. Its swings can be used to keep time, as in a pendulum clock.

pixel
One of the tiny colored squares that makes up an image on a screen.

radioactive
Describes a material that gives off high-energy rays, some of which may be harmful.

robot probe
An unmanned spacecraft that is designed to explore other planets, asteroids, or moons.

rune
One of the letters of the Germanic alphabet. Some runes were thought to have magical powers, like spells.

semaphore
Way to communicate messages visually using two lengths of wood, flags, or the operator's own arms. Different positions indicate different letters or words.

smelt
Heating ore to separate the metal from the rock.

supersonic
Traveling faster than the speed of sound, which is about 650 mph (1,040 km/h) for aircraft.

telegraph
Way to send messages long-distance, usually by sending electrical signals along a wire.

telepathically
Communicating from mind to mind, without words.

vibration
A fast movement that makes something shake or wobble from side to side.

vulcanize
To add sulfur to a material to make it more elastic and stronger.

wire-frame object
A 3-D computer model that looks as if it has been made from wire and provides the basic shape for virtual designs.